Afro Soul

NEHEMY N. KIHARA

ISBN:1539058050

ISBN-13: **978-1539058052**

DEDICATION

To all the children of Africa and the descendants from this

cradle of all humanity.

Also dedicated to Pan-Africanist Professor and founder of the Religious

Heritage of the African World, ITC, Clack Atlanta University Complex, the

late Dr. Tofori-Atta G. B. Thomas , an African-American whose love for

Congo, made him a great Pan-African Church leader and Scholar.

Dedicated also to all my Maa ancetors ,

Laikipiak Maasai ,Il-Chamus ,Sampur and the Sa(Tha)gishu- Agikuyu

,relatives of Akamba,Ameeru,Aembu and Segeju ,who interacted and

intermarried with them in the plains of Laikipia, to produce the Kenyan

Pan-Africanist, that I became

.

CONTENTS

ACKNOWLEDGMENTS

I acknowledge Anne Baksheevs, a Russian-Canadian violinist and

ethnomusicologist for her constant support and encouragement to

get the ideas into a book.

She also taught me the similarities of Eastern Europeans and

people of African descent. She reminded me in a humor mood, the

paleontological scientific fact that

'Beyond all of our assumed differences;

We are all originally Africans.

Julie Wanjiru Kaiga, for her excitement

And encouragement when I shared what I was writing about.

Also for her insights into

the Pan-African World.

1 INTRODUCTION

A. Scope

The topics that are treated in this book are those that the writer feels can capture the intention of the continuous research being done or will be done by others on this subject and in the specific areas under consideration.

By drawing on the literature available this writer therefore will generalizes his findings to develop broad surveys.

However, since there are interrelationship among the various elements in the subjects treated, the subdivision suggested cannot therefore escape obvious limitations, despite the methodological attempt to keep up with the accepted order of socio-scientific research.

A.. Research Design

The purpose of the book is both exploratory and descriptive, oriented towards a positive clarification and interpretive explanations of firstly, the distorted images of African Peoples.

Secondly their Socio-cultural and Religious Movements in the World.

Thirdly, to provide material and literature for further discussion and research.

However, the writer feels that he cannot escape dealing with variables in time and space in accordance with the research model whether these are formulated explicitly or not, at least this serves to guide the

In the discussion of the racial concepts of white and black, the writer will lean more on the Darker side of h

Humanity, which will be referred to as Afroz ,and as the ground of his discursive departure, the 'Lighter humanity' will be referred to as the Euroz.

In case the language seems strong enough to offend somebody, take note that no such an offense was intended.

After all, a revolution like the one being suggested henceforth, would not be worthy its cause, if it follows the same path it sets out to clear and clarify.

Hence it is not just a matter of cultural chauvinism or putting any guilt feelings on the lighter pinkish Euroz, but it is a question of survival of "the most humiliated of peoples in recent times, namely the darker brownish Afroz.

2 DARKER HUMANITY

The Darker Peoples

When one thinks of the `Darker Peoples' especially in the United States of America, there is always a danger of limiting that category to the people whom the 'Lighter people' after enslaving from their motherland of Africa baptized in Spanish `as the Negroes'.

Basically the word `Black' or concept is not for them self-explanatory as assumed, for it applies to a people whose skin pigment is beautifully brownish, darker as the universe in which the Creator placed them.

 Black however, as a symbol and color has been misused and misplaced than any other color because in the world of art, literature, drama and religion it stands for death, sorrow and agony.

Moreover, it is in darkness that God chose to create Nature and in His image, our "Darker and Lighter Humanity". Unfortunately, in places like Africa, the color was used and interpreted in the educational symbol of the writing Black Board and the white chalk.

This writer still remembers as a young boy in school, when a lighter Euroz missionary cum educator teaching the African students said that, "this is a black Board it is wide and big, but useless without this tiny small white chalk".!

Then repeatedly the students were asked to repeat those words after his assuming and cunning question;

"What Color makes black meaningful and useful?"

As expected the students helplessly and effortlessly replied

"Sir, it is the white in the chalk"

Then proudly as he walks in front of them he says

"Black Students repeat again!! With me 'Without the white black is nothing!!'"

And like in any other classroom the students did so.

This author vividly recalls such incidents and his memory painfully documents these twisted lies, coated as facts, which show us clearly what the lighter pinkish pigmented Europeans created by distorted the darker brownish pigmented African self-images in the pretext of learning ,in the educational system that they created.

In the field of religion these lighter peoples henceforth referred as Euroz , instead of whites, supposed to represent purity, distorting the whole image of purity as a virtue, making it to represent their race.

Thus it was to be assumed that when a clergy puts on a Black cassock, the white clerical collar on his neck is supposed symbolically , to purify the black and sinful world.

It is this sort of misuse of the color that made it possible in the pretext of beauty, for the Euroz to introduce cosmetics which many darker Afroz women, before they discovered the folly, grasped with interest and in speed so as to look like the lighter Euroz.

What the author is attempting to illustrate here, is to how Black as a color or concept has been misused. The current dictionaries too give the same idea of Black as bad and evil, representing only the worst.

However, there is beauty in darkness, without it we could not have the lighter side. According to the Bible, in Genesis we are told that God create light from darkness.

Thus in the beginning and hopefully in infinity darkness is also an image of God.

It is this concept that this author chooses to use in this book.

Realizing altogether that the people defined `white' are not as white as snow, for that race can still be characterized by the same definitions that they have been used for the so called 'black' race.

After all slavery in the America is still a reminder of their historical racial hostility, evil and inhuman nature. Nor are the so called 'black' an extract of coal.

Unfortunately coming from the dust of the ground and from old Adam and Eve no race in the world can claim `ethnic purity' in thought and deed, yet in Rhodesia, South Africa and Namibia and other parts of liberated Africa the claim was once and still is alive and sound to a lesser degree.

Revealing of course within what is supposed to represent purity an angry devilish motive and purpose advocated by these crude racial bigots, terrorists and thugs.

The author is re-defining and dismissing `white versus black' conceptualization and does not care running against the dictionaries that are written from a Euroz mind.

The author affirms that he is Afroz and created in God's image, as such, he has the human right given since birth to redefine in existence what the global `Afro Soul' is about and what he is as a person.

That is the purpose of this book or the research in general; to specifically "dig as in a distorted mine ground, a philosophical-religious truth with the light of the cultural and historical dimensions of the "African Peoples".

The story of the Afroz has been confused with criminalized blackness and white wash of politics, economics, religion, literature, music and education.

This author agrees with Dr. James Costen a former Moderator of the Presbyterian Church, USA, Dean of Interdenominational Theological Center and Johnson C. Smith Seminary in Atlanta, when he said in his paper `Black Presbyterianism; Yesterday Today and Tomorrow' that,

"No greater tool of enslavement can be utilized than to rob a person his sense of history and the significance of his present contribution."

Indeed, that was and is what is happening, Afroz heritage has been overcoated and confused with that of the Greeks, Babylonians, Romans, English and other Euroz, through exploitation,abuse and misinterpretation.

Our motherland of Africa has been shifted, redistributed divided and polluted to satisfy the Euroz selfish hunger and greed to rule what they called the `dark continent.' of Africa.

It is the same image of a Beautiful Continent that they abuse in the movies and in the language used in the mass media, where the word `terrorists' substitutes for an eager and honest

African freedom fighters. These struggled in the lonely jungles, forests, deserts or mountains for the liberation of his brothers and sisters in the yoke of bondage under some European assumed to be their master.

Tarzan as a white master dominates the movie scenes with his white colleagues as the jungle lords, without whose presence jungle life could be no more.

Moreover it is such misunderstandings that this book attempts to clarify ,within its limitations and less of the observation of the Euroz yardstick of scholarship and language.

We attempt by examining the Afroz understanding of Theology and Anthropology, that is of God as the Creator and the emergence of supportive social organization, religious movements, its leaders and culture. Starting from their motherland of Africa, into the Diaspora of the Afro-World (the Caribbean, Central and South America).

3 AFRICAN BELIEF AND SOCIAL SYSTEMS

When an Afroz person confesses that s/he is created in God's image, that statement stands firm as an affirmation of faith, any reasonable person cannot start uncalled for debate by arguing the opposite. Through an excuse of ignorance such a person can be forgiven.

The reason why such a statement stands firm as a fact is because the Afroz story and heritage undistorted reveals the religious consciousness of the people.

No wonder the world re-known Professor John Mbiti, one of African's leading theologians says (after examining a great and vast number of African societies) that "the African is notoriously religious."

An examination of the African cultures and societies, where every Afroz person claims their ancestry supports such a claim. Even most of the Euroz sociologists,

Anthropologists and theologians in search of knowledge and in most cases fame, in Africa, cannot help despite their racial eyes to agree with that undisputable fact. To those we offer a smile as the writer quotes them in later pages.

It is interesting that the journalists Emory and Myrta Ross conclude their book 'the African' disturbed by the Biblical words of Luke 17:21 "Behold the Kingdom of God is within you." Revealed indeed an observation that all of us would conclude while addressing ourselves to the religious heritage of the Afroz People.

For indeed despite the disturbance the Euroz people brought to Africa the Afroz people can still look at the mountains and hills from where their existence and survival comes from and say "we know whom we believe and we know He is able."

To use the words of Chinua Achebe an African novelist when "Things fall apart",4 the Black person is able to

preserve the ruins of his village and heritage no matter what the white person sets on motion.

Like deep waters, the heart of the Black still keeps that heritage alive, for the society still maintains honor and respect for the "Almighty."

For even when the pinkish Euroz missionary arrived he did not have to bring a new name for God, for before he came to Africa God was still there as an existential reality, he has been within the society, moving amongst the people ages immemorial.

Another Euroz couple Simon and Phoebe Ottenberg in `Cultures and Societies of Africa' make a very important point by saying that "Often the organization of the gods or spirits in a religion parallel s that of the human society".

Although this author have some problems with their use of the name `Gods' instead of spirits especially when they say: there are different types and functions of spirits, there is also a variation in the interrelations between deities in African religious

systems.

In some there are complex pantheons of Gods, headed by a high God who is often the creator, with a number of gods, smaller gods and sometimes minor spirits. In relationships often assigned to the members within a Parthenon.

Deities are designated as Gods or spirits according to their relative power and sometimes, whether they have human form or not.A system may include one or both types.

Despite such problem which arise from their conceptualization and anthropological point of view they indeed confirm in their view the African religious heritage in question, as being deeply rooted in society.

4 AFRICAN CULTURAL HERITAGE

The Black Religious heritage is not only confirmed by the societal

organization but is revealed by the cultural systems too.

While this writer disagrees with some of the sweep of generalizations in Continuity and Change in African Cultures by William R. Bastom and Melville J. Herskivits, their definition of culture is of course impressive.

Culture rather than social institution, is what distinguishes man from the rest of the biological world. Other animals and insects as well, have societies, but only man uses language, manufactures tools, and possesses art, religion, and other aspects of culture.

The concern with culture rather than with society and social institutions thus emphasizes the specifically human elements of man's behavior.

Further these authors agree that "despite the intensity of Christian Missionary effort and the thousand years of Moslem proselytizing which has worked in the history of various parts of Africa, religion continue to manifest vitality everywhere."7.

The religious movements of the Black people manifest themselves everywhere assuring the world that the African culture in its religious aspect is here to stay as it has been over the centuries.

The Afroz Islanders of the Caribbean, the Latino `Afroz' of South America or those in Central America or in the United States confirms this

These people, still , after years of harsh conditions of acculturation under slavery their religion still flourishes despite the forces and challenges of urbanization and industrialization.

Of course one may rightly contend that there are cultural differences and contrasts but through observation of fellow Africans from different parts of the motherland and those of the diaspora there are undoubtedly underlying similarities.

Today in the writings or literature of the Afroz writers and artists one can see clearly their production of forms and patterns which are a part of the culture, as they react to their societies, religious, political and economic institutions, they indeed are struggling to give meaning, values and stability amid change.

Thus Ngugi Wa Thiongo in his novel Homecoming writes:

'For we must strive for a form of social organization that will face the manded spirit and energy of our people so we can build a new country and sing a new song, perhaps in a small way the African writer can help in articulating the feelings behind this struggle.'

This Afroz Religious Heritage as it is seen in the cultural manifestations of the Afro Societies, can be to the Afroz People (to use the words of Professor Alan Ogot and Rev. F.B. Welbourn) "A place to feel at home."

Both of the above authors in their study of the independent churches in East Africa, say that,

"If a home is destroyed whether the material house or the relationship between those who inhabit it, a new home must be found or its individual members become insecure, maladjustment, alien society.

If they are unlucky they go to the wall, if lucky they build for themselves afresh".

This writer agrees with the authors as they continue, that under the impact both the structure and the relationship of tribal society were destroyed however this writer disagree with their conclusion that "with them the myth that held them together and was upheld

by them was destroyed."

To this writer the struggle still goes on, deep in the culture and the society the religious consciousness and heritage is still alive and manifests itself in different forms of movements today.

With Oginga Odinga this writer agrees that it is "Not Yet Uhuru"(freedom)

We must strive to attain the freedom and the independence that makes us build on our Afroz religious heritage, so that we can get a real meaningful freedom and achievement in our economic, political and cultural spheres of existence as a Afro people.

Addressing himself to the same question Dr. Tofori - Atta, Professor of Church and Society and Director of the Religious Heritage of the African World at the Interdenominational Theological Center, Atlanta) concludes in a Lenten devotional booklet series (liberation and unity) that ... "and the struggle goes on until our soul-gram comes."

Indeed the Black people are involved in a struggle, we may have a long way to go, for not only have we to go against the known European distorted "Black or African history" but we must correct and rewrite it a new or afresh.

We must bring it to a position, where our culture and religious consciousness speaks for itself.

So that the `African peoples' in the homeland of Africa and those in the `Diaspora' in the Afro world either in the United States of America, Europe, Asia, the Islands of Caribbean or in the Central and South America may be seen in their rightful perspective.

These share the same humanity, a humanity that has experienced intensive manipulation, these claim their ancestry "only in Africa" where the Black experience begun and must be centered. languages indeed it is a land of Africa.

5 MOTHERLAND AFRICA

Just as they disturbed and distorted the image of the Afroz people.,the Euroz disturbed also the Afroz homeland which they divided and ruled under the "yoke of Colonialism."

There are many who argue that the advent of Europeans powers in the continent of Africa saw slavery come to an end, but only to the extent of exporting Africans:

The European colonizers continued the process of slavery and in the form of cheap labor in the farm or lands that the Euroz settlers had stolen from the indigenous populations.

A lot of positive things that came out of this situation, makes the African still to believe God who was there from the very beginning is still at work.

The Euroz subjected the Afroz to their assumed racial supremacy, forcefully demanding total servitude. They seem to have forgotten that it is only the One Lord God ,the Almighty Creator who is worthy such a submission.

For it is only Him who is the Supreme head of the universe including the Motherland of Africa.. Moreover, this motherland despite her deep religious heritage has been in a state of tumult, the dawn of colonialism, that confuses the whole question of religion.

The whole sphere of African faith has been challenged. In his book African Nationalism, Rev. Ndambaningi Sithole, the Zimbabwe Politician and United Church of Christ Minister says:

`Faith is part and parcel of human life on all levels. The interpretation of the nature and destiny of man depends upon the kind of faith. Hence a Godless faith tends to devalue man, and man is finally held accountable to the earthly-power-that-be.

He further contends that, The use of the industrial system, and all that goes with it, has destroyed many religious conceptions which gave content to African life, and has thereby created a religious vacuum.

Further he defines what he means by saying that, "A religious vacuum means a state of godlessness, and this in turn threatens African life with hollowness, emptiness and meaninglessness, for indeed, man shall not live by bread alone but every word which comes from the mouth of God.

This was said twenty centuries ago, and it is still true today. There is that hunger for God, for things more abiding."

These indeed are words worthy quoting for they point not only to at a crisis but also point at a need, a need for religious fulfilment and completeness not only in the motherland but even in the Diaspora. We must also bear in mind that the Motherland of course is a Continent occupying an area of 11,506,000 square miles, 20% of the earth with a population of over a billion, which is 15% of the world's total population.

Total. Global Percentage of Adherents of Religion

African Traditional religions	100 million	1.40%
Bahá'í	7.0 million	0.10%
Buddhism	376 million	5.25%
Cao Dai	4.0 million	0.06%
Chinese traditional religion[c]	394 million	5.50%
Christianity	2.2 billion[3]	31.50%

Ethnic religions excluding some in separate categories

	300 million	4.19%
Hinduism	1 billion	13.95%
Islam	1.6 billion[4]	22.32%
Jainism	4.2 million	0.06%
Judaism	14 million	0.20%
Neo-Paganism	1.0 million	0.01%
Rastafarianism	0.6 million	0.01%
Secular[a]/Nonreligious[b]/Agnostic/Atheist	≤1.1 billion	15.35%
Shinto	4.0 million	0.06%

Sikhism	23 million	0.32%
Spiritism	15 million	0.21%
Tenrikyo	2.0 million	0.02%
Unitarian Universalism	0.8 million	0.01%
Zoroastrianism	2.6 million	0.04%
Total 7167 Billion		100%

The total distribution of the religious population is given in 1975 Encyclopedia Britannica Book of the year as follows.

Total Christians	-	2 billion (31.50%)
Eastern Orthodox	-	
Roman Catholics	-	
Protestant	-	
Judaism	-	14m(0.20%)
Muslim	-	1.6 b (22.32%)
Zoroastrian	-	2.6m (0.4%)
Chinese Traditional Religions	--	394m(5.50%)
Sikhism		-23m (
Shinto	-	4m(0.06%)

Ethnic Religions   300m(

African Traditional Religion   100m(1.40%)

Taoist   -   0

Confucian   500

Buddist   -   2,000

Hindu   -   1b.(

TOTAL   198,909,440

The distribution of the total "Black" darker skinned populations' percentage in the World is discussed elsewhere. It is worth noting that the Motherland of Africa contains about 50 different nations or more (when Islands are included)

These nations have diversity of more than 1,000 Lingual-ethnic communities (defined by the Euroz scholars as tribes) who speak almost an equal number of languages indeed it is a land of contrasts flowing with honey and milk. , but due to unequal distribution many live in poverty.

An attempt to present these countries is made here so that one can look at the sketch map provided and locate the country mentioned.

These countries are grouped according to the divisions that are mostly used for classification. That is Northern, Western, Central, Eastern, Southern and some islands are presented especially as former Portuguese colonies to territories which are now independent. Those still under foreign influence and dominion either Spain, French and British are at the verge of independence, there is no attempt made to isolate such, they are included in their appropriate location.

Map of Africa

6 DIASPORIC GLOBAL AFROZ

It is unfair to speak or confine the Afroz peoples only to their motherland "Africa" for their "Diaspora" extends into the whole world, therefore forming what has come to be known as the Afro-world.

This world extends from the United States of America, where most of the Afroz people were transported as slaves; these are estimated to be more than 48 million in the states alone to date (16% of total population).

The other continent where a great number of Afroz people exist is in the South America, Central America and the Caribbean where such Black Republics like Haiti Still speaks to the fact of the vastness and teeming diversity of the African heritage here.

The Afro-world is unique, in that it is both trans-Saharan (including the Semitic lingual-ethnics of North Africa) and trans-Atlantic in that it includes the Afroz people who in some cases have been mixed up with the Indoz of the Islands in the Caribbean Sea, Asia, North Africa and also Europe.

According to the late Prof. Ali Mazrui; " this adds new dimensions to black destiny and its place in a world federation cultures"

In his book World Culture and the Black experience Mazrui, concludes that he sought to demonstrate the issues involved in decolonizing and the Black intellect and enhancing its innovative capability a language from other cultures might be invited to serve the destiny of societies far from its origins.

A science developed by others may provide shoulders for black "Newtons" to stand on and see further afield. A religion springing from a different civilization could be made to confront true black experience itself. Let us again repeat "In the beginning was the word, and the word was God". But was God Black?

This timely observation from the Kenyan and one of World's leading political scientists is appropriate for our understanding of the Afro world. He contends further that,

The whole of Black destiny may be a search for a new answer to that question, a trans-valuation of values that would end the imagery of negation that has hung over the concept of blackness and would restore the Blackman to the mainstream of human history."

This writer agree with Mazrui that such advantages of language as English, French, Spanish, Arabic and both Swahili and Hausa should be utilized to overcome the barriers that disunite the Afro world.

In the Afroz experience we come to understand the existence of the Diaspora of the African people and their cultural cousins who manifest themselves in the emergence of the third World (or the shadow of the fourth world if it exists).

It is this world beyond the Pan-Africanism that people like the late Kenyan economist/politician Tom Mboya tended to defend when they spoke of Pan-Africanism as a non-racial organization.

As said elsewhere in the Afro world the "Afroz Diaspora" consciousness is expressed by the writers such as the Jamaican Marcus Garvey, George Padmore, Aime Casaire, and the Guyanese writer E.E. Braithwaite who had questioned himself of the consciousness by Sayre was there a part of me that remained African after all these years.

C.L.R. James in a kind of homecoming (p. 49) contends that "before they could begin to see themselves as free and independent people they had to clear their minds and the stigma that African was inherently inferior and degraded."

It is such writers that the Diaspora or the Afro-world is making itself known as alive and sound in the Global context..

Therefore, it is appropriate to mention that the Afro-world as an extension from the motherland is involved in the struggle for identity as an issue that had caused the former Moderator Rt. Rev. John Gatu,(1972) then Chairman of the (A.A.C.C.) All African Conference of Churches and also General Secretary of the Presbyterian Church of East Africa) to call temporarily stoppage of western missionaries.

The 5 year period moratorium proposed a withdrawal of the foreign missionaries from the third world-, which would allow the people to find their own selfhood and plan their own futures.

The identity of the Afro-world however have been found in the search of selfhood--which is the Afroz experience
which assures the Black people of whom Franz Fanon speaks of, as the "Wretched of the Earth" to find their place in the universe.

In the Negro Almanac, by Harry Ploski,(1974) `The Black experience' is presented to a length. However, one of the things worth noting here is that the Afro-world as it manifests itself in the continent of South America
It can still be traced, in the sense that most of the Africans who came here in the early 17th and 18th century still retain much of their heritage or Africanism, a very important consciousness that no one ought to overlook lest s/he forget their native land.

These people may speak English, French, Spanish, Portuguese, Italian or Hindi. Yet they are the Global Diaspora of the Africans. An attempt is made here to give the countries that they exists in mainly in the Caribbean, the Central and South America.

Altogether the author attempts to give the percentage in the more than 40 countries, of the Afroz Diaspora. This reveals indeed that in such places like Columbia 8%, Equator 6%, Uruguay 5%, Venezuela 10%, where most people assume there are no Afroz, their presence is strong and growing. As many people self – identify as Afro-latinoz.

7 THE AFRICAN RELIGIOUS MOVEMENTS

In the past religion for the African people was integrated with their whole life. Beliefs and practices that were significant to life were the social experiences in which religion manifested itself. The whole question of morality, daily living and all rituals in the society were made meaningful by the religious ceremonies.

It was from this social organization, which by nature was religious that the individuals got their values and dignity. It is here that culture molded and formed humans to be God-honoring individuals, therefore producing a religious centered society.

The religious movements existed to the extent that they were rooted in the peoples' lives and souls. It is in their conscience that the word of God was written, through childhood these acquired the necessary instruction and teaching, concerning what the society under the Almighty Creator requires of the individual members.

The land and its soil which gave people food that they consumed ,and in which they were buried after death, were of vital importance just as the universe for these too were manifestations of God.

In his book Facing Mount Kenya the late founding President of Kenya Mzee Jomo Kenyatta writing about the (Agikuyu-slightly above a quarter of all Kenyans) Africans concludes that,

"The African is conditioned by cultural and social institutions of centuries, to a freedom of which Europe has little conception, and it is not in his nature to accept seldom forever.

He realizes that he must fight unceasingly for his own complete emancipation, for without this he is doomed to remain the prey of rival imperialisms which in every successive year will drive their fangs move deeply into his vitality and strength."

That worth quotation from one of Africa's leading statesmen `the once old wise one' explains the fact that the African throughout the centuries had a deep religious heritage and consciousness, strange and unknown to the Euroz people , no wonder than that they brought Christianity and presented it in a way that it looked as if it is "made in Europe" or made of the white[pinkish] color which they had pasted on it.

One of the modern Anglo- Euroz missionaries Donald Jacobs in his book, African Culture and African Church admits this when he says that," We should not be surprised to find the gospel as brought to Africa by modern missionary movement had a western tint, for western missionaries had to speak out of their experience. They had no other."

Unfortunately most of the pinkish Euroz people have not admitted a similar self- excuse. We may all agree with that, however, they should have taken their time to learn before they bulldozed other peoples "Ground of Being".

However, Don Jacobs puts this well when he further admits,

"Unfortunately at the beginning of the century, because of the new tools and weapons he had developed, the western man felt culturally superior and looked upon the non-white world in a patronizing way. And missionaries were not free of this though we had problems with it.. To be sure, we were a bit slow to listen to the wisdom of the non-white world"

The Euroz because of not taking time to listen misinterpreted much of the African religious heritage. It was and is a known fact that pre-Christianity the Afro religious movement was based on a "Supreme Monotheism".

It is also agreed by the majority of Afroz theologians and Bible scholars that there is a possibility that the Old Testament Hebrews during their time in Egypt (then unpolluted by the Greeks and Babylonian Polytheism and Pantheism, acquired the monotheistic revelation of what they came to understand as the only Lord and Living God.

After and before they came to Egypt they were idol worshippers and polytheistic, a tendency that used to crop up now and then, even at the time they were in the wilderness, note that this was their greatest temptation and sin, was that of creating graven images or idols and worshipping them.

One of Africa's foremost Nigerian theologian Bolaji Idowu (1967) says that "Africa recognizes only one God, the Supreme Universal God, even though she has pictures of Him which are of various shades, calls Him by various names and approaches Him in various ways; He nevertheless remains one and the same God the creator of all the end of the earth."

It is unfortunate, however that most of the Euroz scholars and writers who have written on `African Societies' their cultures and religion. Mostly because of western pride of considering themselves as specialists or experts on Africa, Probably because they happened to visit there or have stayed there for a time, have tended to lack completely what Professor Bolaji Idowu calls `the scholar's highway code of caution, openness sympathy and reverence".

Therefore, because of such a preconception and misconception instead of approaching African Traditional Religion with caution as that which gives the darker persons basic norm of behavior.

They have treated it as fossils, not only distorting the whole base of the Afroz human nature and personality but also the spirit.

That is why the whole field of our tradition or heritage form our Afroz past sounds so messed up. We now know of course that, that someone who over the centuries has been messing up our religion, are the "pink-ones" or the Euroz.

Now our task is to uncover much of our indigenous heritage from the dust the Euroz tried to bury it with. Such a research to trace the African religious movements is a heavy task and equally desirable in a time like now when the Afroz is struggling to put his own history on the right focus, basing of course the center of the universe in the Afro-world and Africa instead of Europe.

Struggling with the same question and task the AMECEA a Catholic Church Association, meeting in Uganda (at Gaba Institute) came up with five interlocutors which this writer thinks would be helpful in our understanding of the religious movements as they manifest themselves in the religiously pluralistic society in Africa or in the Afro-world.

The interlocutors were identified as:

"1.The religious specialist, priest, shrine keeper, spirit medium and doctor.

2. The great religious personality whose harmony is cherished by people living today.

3. There is the Christian who feels an unresolved duality in himself, having been baptized into a church which does not recognize the existence of a coherent system of African traditional beliefs that he must repudiate or come in terms with.

4. Members of the independent church or neo-traditional movements which is often originated in a failure or absence of a dialogue.

5. Finally, sophisticated people with submerged traditional values, but who need a theological approach to modern socio-political problems"

It is interesting to note that the five categories mentioned are quite adequate for our study. Although this writer's observation of Christianity or such religions based on great spiritual personalities not only fit here but cross-fertilize and come into dialogue with the African indigenous religion.

An observation in South-Central America and the Caribbean show that the African folk music still marvels that southern Continent for "It reveals the African style traditional heritage and consciousness. Yet deep inside its soul, exists the religiousness of the motherland like a might drum sounds dynamically and clearly."

Therefore, like in Africa of old, here the Afro-religion still possess the rituals, cults, and patterns connecting the individual not only to the cosmic motherland and world but nature as a whole and above all else to the Almighty God.

"Seen this way religion or in this context stands for an apprehension of reality across the whole field of life. This was the explanatory apprehension that produced its mandatory force; out of it, in one way or another, there emerged what may reasonably be called a science of social control".

Such a religion that the author describes, is what we would learn as the Afro-world's religious consciousness, that had controlled the African's destiny during their time of struggle throughout the centuries.

Mary Slater(1968) in the Caribbean Islands says that "The slaves brought not only their songs and dances but also their superstitions and religion: shango and vodoo, they brought folklore, Anansi, the spider-man who's Puckish exploits runs throughout many Island tales, deriving from Africa rather than Jamaica where he had become almost a national sprite."

The same writer continues elsewhere that during the period of emancipation after the slaves were set free that "this was the beginning of the smiling people throughout the islands."

The point here is that after all the oppression the Afroz experienced, his religion after years in a strange land of different tongues and kindred was able to take form either as in the Shango and Vodoo the most dominant religious movements in the Caribbean. It is these that have formed the essence of the Caribbean culture and the endurance of that Afroz soul.

Speaking of the Caribbean culture in a country like Surinam, African musical forms are still intact. In Cuba, the Afro-Cuban music still flourishes in the African heritage and rhythm.

The Afro Puerto-Rican plena and other forms of the African music of which a former CIA spy cum Travel Expert- Eugene Fodor(1972) said, "out of the plantations stalks ball room came the drums of Africa, rhumba, boor, conga the guaracha and the malate".

The other thing that amazes all of us is that in the Afroz Republic of Haiti, Bahamas, Bermuda, Minogue, Dominican, Martinique, Guadeloupe and in all other parts of the Afro-world either in the Caribbean, Central or South America, the African tongue was able to penetrate Latin, French, English and Spanish languages and still create itself a new in such a tongue as the Cwelo (Creole) as an Afro-French dialect.

This can be called truly the essence of the Afro-culture. Fodor explains that the Caribbean culture "is adaptive, inventing and full of `jure de voile' which transcends race, color and previous conditions of servitude".

It is no wonder that most of the people who have visited the Caribbean Islands are marveled by the hospitality of these people.

These indeed have the Afro-soul. The term 'Afroz Soulz' as conceptualized by this writer is a philosophical attempt by a grassroots theologian/philosopher to explain the essence of the African religious movements and heritage in the context of the African world. No wonder DuBois(1903) had already capture the concept in his Souls of the Negro Folk.

Having therefore examined the African Religious movements as they had expressed themselves in the past (Zamani in Swahili), let us now turn to the present (Sasa in Swahili) to examine how these religious movements express or manifest themselves in other religious such as in Christianity or Islam in general.

An observation in Africa reveals that one of the impressively flourishing religious movement is that of the "Prophet". **South of the Sahar**a especially, such movements as that of the prophetess Alice Lishina, a former Presbyterian and founder of the Lumba Movement of Zambia, had been under persecution for their threat to the established Government.

This movement made a big impact in the neighboring nations of Malawi, Zaire, Ruanda Burundi, Zimbabwe and South Africa during the early 1960's, under the leadership of the Prophetess.

In **West Africa**, in Nigeria Isaac Babalole Akinyele's Christ Apostolic Church of which he was the President made a great impact in the Yorubaland.

While the Church of the Lord Arandula Movement spread all over Nigeria and in Liberia, Sierra Leone and other neighboring countries and has sent missionaries to England where an office and branch is established in London.

This author had an opportunity of meeting for lunch with the leaders in 1975 in Atlanta, Georgia ;where he learned of their soon mission to send more Missionaries to the United States of America and all over the world.

In **Central Africa**, the Kibanguist Church emerged in in the nation of Zaire from a former Baptist healing and anti-witch craft Movements in the Continent.

In **East Africa**, Zacharia Kivuli High Priest and the founder the African Israel Church, Nineveh is yet another example of such movements (and the goals they had for the movement reveal an extensive mobilization and expansion.

This author remembers attending College with one of his good friends, Isaac Kivuli, who is the son of Church founding Bishop Kivuli, Sr.; and later teaching 'theological education by extension' to their leaders at the Nineveh Headquarters at Jebrok in Vihiga County, Western Kenya; which was under the leadership of the youthful Archbishop Kivuli III. and his wife who is also a Co-Leader of the Church..

Another level under which the Afro Religious movements are flourishing can be seen in the Oba Peter's movement of a fishing community in Niger Delta called the "Aiyetoro" the Cherubim and Seraphim society composed of harbingers as its main membership.

The Mau Mau Movement of Kenya, (seen by the western world even today as he bloodiest "Guerilla Movement" in history) although a political vehicle to achieve freedom; expressed its religious practices through the apparatus of oath taking ceremonies.

Oath taking is typical to the traditional society which as a result was ensured by a fanatical obedience. More research need to be done on other similar Guerilla Movements, such as Frelimo of Mozambique and the Anya Anya of Sudan, for a similar tendency may have been practiced.

Yet another arena of African religious movements is the political. An example would be the Ghanaian Convention Peoples Party . Under the leadership of the "consciousness" philosopher Kwame Nkrumah, it had devised not only a creed, hymns and prayers centered on Kwame Nkrumah..

He was the person of "Osagyefo" warrior chief, who saved the nation, thus expressing a deep religious yearning and consciousness.

A similar situation had risen in the **North-Central African** nation of Chad where the Elderly President 'Emperor' Bokassa wanted and almost succeeded in making himself a "god image" only to meet his death after a coup .

Later same situations developed in the Zairean "Mobutism" under General Joseph Desire Sese Seko's Mobutu's personality, and the movement towards a political attempt to capture the people's religious consciousness in the person of the leader or head of State. In fact most of the African states have been on the verge of this sort of extremism which has its consequences at the end and in most cases after one such a leader almost reaches the apex of the "glory" he desires.

 In **North Africa**, a different situation exists in that while only a small Christian minority flourishes, mostly in the Coptic Church, the Islam Religion in its various manifestations seems to have swallowed up or captured the people's culture. Yet under the challenges of such new political forms like the "Scientific Socialism" in Ethiopia and Somalia.

The participation of the Christian and traditional religion of the South Sudan, there might be coming another dimension of the Black Religious Movement or the Afro Soul.

The future of the African Religious movements seem promising as long as there exists the need for God the Almighty. It is in this inescapable image, Afroz were created.

This image may be called or classified by the Euroz world as animism or paganism, yet such concepts are meaningless when the Afro-soul is firmly rooted on this Ground of Being.

It is this reality that this author's once teacher/principal at St Pauls' University-United Theological College- Professor. Samuel Kibicho of the University of Nairobi spoke of in his article on African Traditional Religion and Christianity speaking particularly of the Agikuyu-Africans said:

"As regards God's nature they (the Africans) never tried to theorize about his attributes, they simply experienced his presence. They knew from experience that he has a being completely different from men."

8 PRESERVATION BY DOCUMENTATION

Having seen already that the Afro-world Religious Movements are still manifesting themselves all over, then we can agree with Melville Herskovits in "The Myth of the Negro Past where he takes the position that African survivals can be found in numerous phases of Negro life in the United States.

Supporting the same view is Harry V. Richardson the former President of the Interdenominational Theological Center, Atlanta, Georgia, who maintains that the Africans were inclined to accept Christianity since they already possessed a highly developed religious tradition of their own.

In contrast to these two views we find Franklin Frazier's generalization of which we may not agree with, as he states that "as fact that the enslaved African Negro was practically stripped of his social heritage and indicates likewise.

That it would be difficult to establish any relationship between African religious practices and Negro church which developed on America soil. In his book on The Negro Church in America., he also stated in the beginning, in the book, that an attempt is made to present a general survey and identification of the religious movements of the Afroz people.

Unlike most of the Euroz scholars and writers, the writer does not come to the same conclusions. However this author is indebted to a few, who are quoted because of their relative or intensive research.

Unfortunately just as they did in Africa the Euroz Christians this time in the United States of America communicated to the African Diaspora a message distorted by insidious racism and compromised self-concept and economic self-interest.

No wonder then that such an Afroz Scholar as C. Eric Lincoln concludes in an article on the `Genesis of the Black religious experience in America' by saying that "it was an experience which did much to shape the destinies and to set us firmly on the trend mill which covers the same ground.

Year after year, century after century and from which Black Christians have so recently lavished a final effort to disengage.

All over the Afro world the disengagement process is in motion, the Christianity that was presented with ignorance of the cultural heritage with a deep faith in God now finds itself under the challenge of its authenticity. The European missionaries Christianized Africa but now the call is for the Afroz to Africanize Christianity. That is to make it authentic in the African culture.

One of Africa's well known sociologist and a former President of Ghana, Dr. K.A. Busia, warned that "For conversion to the Christian faith is to be more than superficial, the Christian Church must come to grips with traditional beliefs and practices and with the world view that these beliefs and practices imply."

What Dr. Busia was trying to give a timely warning which he conceived during his research as an African Christian. It is a warning that we should heed.

This author's once history teacher at St. Paul's United Theological College [now St. Paul's University] at Limuru, Kenya, T.A. Beetham, a British Methodist Clergy, in his book, Christianity and New Africa supports Busia's position when he insists that "the word became flesh which lies at the center of the Christian faith must forever be held in together in tension.

This tension is necessary in order not to lose sight of the fact that faith delivered to the saints is all eternal word of God, unchangeable, the manifestation of that word was in the flesh of a man of the Jewish people in the first century A.D.

In other words while there can be only one theology, if the word is to incarnate for each people and generation and if it is in every generation to be touched and handled so as to be universally recognized, it must be incarnate in the language and life of the people.

So as for Christianity and Islam, therefore to be meaningful they must be incarnated, a thing that is only central in Christianity which in order to produce a balanced Afroz Religious movement in the future, must come to a dialogue.

The task of Afroz Christians is that of preserving that which made us what we are in essence, that is our religiousness, our belief in the eternal Supreme Creator of which John Mbiti after his study of over three hundred ethnic groups' religious expressions, all these scattered over the African continent substantiates by his conclusion that:

"Without a single exception the people have a notion about God the Supreme Being" God is self-sufficient, self-supporting, self-continuing just as he is self-originating. His spirit is emphasized in part that throughout Africa, there are no images or physical representations of God.

After collecting and rediscovering one's own history, we shall be able to have a better documentation of what we have been, what we are, what becomes of us and what we shall be.

That is our destiny as Afroz and part of Humanity. The author believes and still contends that there is more of our being than we see in the historical books mostly written from the Euroz perspectives.

The Afroz peoples are the hope of the world. That is as the children of Israel, God has been able to work his own purpose on earth through the Africans.

The Euroz world has always meant bad for us as a Afroz people, yet it has all been their own burden (a.k.a .white man's burden).

Our history confirms that we have been used for salvation of other ethnic groups since creation. The writer's discovery of this fact makes him contend that there is a possibility in the future for Afroz to be the world's leader.

Is not the champion of Boxing Sports, Muhammad Ali "the Greatest." Yet in other sports and events the Afroz Greatness is a reality, that the world witnesses in all Olympic Games.

It is the motherland of Africa that saved the children of Israel from a possible death from famine.

Joseph as the Prime Minister in the African Nation of Egypt saved them through the Afroz's grain (Genesis Chapter 4). Jesus Christ as a young child was saved in Africa, where according to God's command his earthly parents made a flight to Egypt, The same African Nation that the Hebrews were saved in.

Yet, on the way to Calvary the Son of God was helped by an Afroz called Simon of Crate to accomplish the salvation mission, almost at a time when he could not go further; God the Almighty choose the Afroz soul Simon for that "special mission of hastening the Beloved son to go through the agony of saving humanity" including the Euroz. Then the wise African visitors in Jerusalem during the Pentecost.

What of the Christian church in its infant years it was the North African Theologians and Philosophers such as Athanasius, Augustine, Cyprian, Clement, Cyprian, Cyril, Dionysius, Origen, Tertullian that saved it from lack of leadership and administration.

David Barret, (1967), Note also that in the scramble for Africa the Euroz world saved itself from shedding its own blood in the quest and greed for power and control as they unfortunately did in the 1st and 2nd World Wars.

No wonder most of them came to Africa with gun in one hand the Bible in the other, cigarettes the cause of certain fatal kinds of cancer as proved by their own scientists, in their mouth and medicine in their hip pockets, crates of beer and liquor in their ships and strict laws against drunkards in their legal diaries and journals.

All this causing a lot of contradiction, confusion, ethnic wars and hatred amongst the Afroz peoples. While asking people to shut their eyes in reverence to God in prayer, they kept their eyes open beholding and coveting the green land yonder, which within a few days they will fence with gun in hand and declare "Private property", "No Black dirty tribals should trespass, this is the white masters' land."

It is this sort of introduction of religiosity that weakened the Christian faith in North Africa so that Islam just came later and got its roots in the peoples culture and flourishes today as a religion of the people.

9 EPILOGUE

In conclusion let us take note that an Anglo-Euroz researcher Dr. David Barret predicted that by A.D. 2000 the African continent will have the largest number of Christians of any continent in the world..

Christianity has undoubtedly become a religion of Africa, and it must be in order to grow. Since it indicates growth we can say it has been a religion of the Afroz people, but still it needs to come into terms with the people's culture.

The word of God speaks to a people as they are. Therefore, to the Afroz person it should address itself to their own situation. To the Euroz and the Asiaz ,it should do the same.

To those doubtful Euroz nationals who still question, whether anything good come from Africa or African traditional religion. The answer of course is yes. Because historically many good things have come not only particularly from the motherland--Africa alone but also from the Afroz world in general and more is on the way.

In times like these when there is a big quest for identity and selfhood it is only the true positive good news that will bring freshness as the eternal word of God is incarnated in the Afroz.

Africans must forgive the Euroz for all the historical evil and injustices that he has done to the Afroz.

It should also be notable that in World Wars, revolutions in France and in the United States, a lot of blood of the Euroz was shed ,for freedom and liberty. In the same battles, enslavement of other humans was questioned, as well as the quest for equality for all.

We are living in an interdependent world in which all human lives matter, because we are all related, despite of our outer or cosmetic differences of our own creation.

However, one thing that remains certain is that as an Afroz scholar, theologian or writer there is a responsibility to put things right, especially to put our-story in the right perspective, centering the experiences of life on our part of humanity, so as to create values and new views of selfhood and destiny.

We have to fight all forms of racism, that is hate that is based on assumptions of prejudice ,that our part of humanity is better, purer and superior than others. We have to do this carefully, so as not to become advocates of reversal discrimination.

For a long time the Euroz or the pink ones have been on the way of Afroz self-development. Yet the time has come to cry to the God of our forefathers, whom the Euroz people struggled to silence, the God who spoke in the thunder and lightning, the same God who gave and still gives rain and crops.

The Afroz experience of suffering has now taken another dimension that of flourishing and awakening with a new hope for survival and salvation for the world, whether in Africa, Latin America, North America, Asia, Europe and Oceania.

All over the global continents Afroz are now scattered. In the western Hemisphere the Afroz face still smiles in kindness and humility.

It is no longer a question of affirming, Negritude or "Nigger-ness' based on our 'pigmentation or quantity of melanin and its basis for our colonization and enslavement by the Euroz.

Our goal and purpose is to humanize the world. To bring us all into appreciating the image of God, in which all humans are created.

The Euroz created in their image the 'Negro' identification,' as was seen in the French Black Code-"Le Code Noir"-What in the world is a Negro ? and why was Spanish language used instead of English or Russian or Gujarat,? .They all have a terms for things that seem black. How come their 'white' self- identification in Spanish is 'blanco' which sounds to most us ,just as black.

Afroz in USA had to undergo through such identifications as savages, slaves, negroes ,fresh water and field/house niggers, and colored, mullatoes and Afro-Americans.

The so called people of color were to be stripped off their humanity so as to be treated like the beasts of the field, that is the donkeys, or the asses and mules.

However, in the new century, in the United States the Afroz eagle flew over and settled in the white house in the form of a son of a Kenyan Afroz, President Barak Obama to show the Afroz are mounting up with wings under God in the new land and in the diaspora.

Yet the struggle is not over, for liberation, justice and freedom forall humanity is still the battle cry. Hopefully, the sound of freedom will continue to ring at the top of Stone Mountain, Georgia as prophesied by Dr. Martin Luther King

.This author has climbed the 1 mile to and 1 mile descend from the top of this great granite Mountain ,so many times. Always feeling the freedom run

Firstly, the Afroz must humbly walk again with our God, our Creator, our Almighty, whose presence in the Universe, the mountains and trees still reminds us that God is our heritage.

We must also note that our Afroz Religious Heritage and Movements are centered on our humanity either one studies religion as a cultural phenomenon or movement, this aspect is unavoidable and of vital importance.

Secondly, there is inadequate written sources by Afroz writers on matters that are of vital important to our selfhood and identity.

We are compelled to use in most cases biased the books written by Euroz scholars , which means the Afroz people must struggle to identify with their religious movements in Africa and Afro-world.

Finally, it is good to note that Afroz heritage and consciousness goes back to the creation of humanity, whether we call it the ` African Genesis' to use Robert Andrey's(1968) words or Genesis of Humanity. The point is that, God still lives, works his purpose and moves in various movements amongst us in our beloved motherland of Africa or its' new lands of the Diaspora in the Afro-world.

Finally, all of us as children of the Almighty Creator must unify and live peacefully with one another.   The world is designed into different geographical and ecological that more or less define our subsistence.

 In these habitats   the Afroz (continental and diaspora); Euroz (continental and diaspora) and Asiaz (continental and diaspora) must co-exist in kindness and sense of love.

10 REFERENCES

1.African Ecclesiastical Review; Volume 16, 1974 p. 427.

2 Achebe,. Chinua , 1958; Things Fall Apart.

London: Heinemann

.

3.Ardrey,Robert ,1967, African Genesis.; A Personal Investigation into Animal Origins and Nature of Man

US; Dell Publishing

4. Barret ,David ,1967 Frontier Situation for Evangelization of Africa; A Survey Report, Nairobi, Kenya, .

5. Bascom, William R.., and Melville J. Herskivits,1959' Continuity and Change in Africa. Boston: William

6.. Beetham,T.A.,1967, Christianity and New Africa.
New York; Frederick A. Prager

7.. Costen Dr. James,1976 Caster, Black Presbyterianism, Yesterday today   and Tomorrow Unpublished paper

8.. Busia. K.A 1971, Search of Democracy in Africa
New York; Frederick A. Prager

9.Davidson,Basil;1969 African Genius, p. 111.

NY: James Curry

10.. Fanon, Frantz ,1963 Wretched of the Earth,

NY; Glove Press

11.DuBois, W.E.B., 1903,Souls of the Black Folks;

Essays and Sketches. Chicago: A.C. McClurg & Co.

12.Fodor,Eugene,1972,Caribbean,BahamasBermuda,p74-77.

Litchfield. Fodor Modern Guides.

13. Herskovits Melville;,1959, The Myth of the Negro Past.

Chicago: University of Chicago Press.

14 .Gatu, John G..1972, "Call to Africanization," AACC Bulletin

November Issue; Nairobi AACC

15. . Idowu, E. Bolaji,1967; The Study of Religion with

SpecialReference to African Traditional Religion, ORITA, p. 12, June

Issue..

16..-------.Ibid,1968; African Tradition Religion,pp16-21. ;London-

.

17..Religious Information the World Almanac, `2016

18. .Jacobs, Donald R., 1972, African Culture and African Church in A New Look at Christianity in Africa, Vol. II No.2.p.5 Geneva: WSCF

.

19.James, C.L.R.,1938; The Black Jacobins. London: Secker &Warburg

20..K .J.V. Bible , Exodus 19:11.

21. Kenyatta,Jomo,1965Facing Mount Kenya; The Tribal life of the Gikuyu, NY; Random House/ Vintage

22. Kibicho, Samuel G.; 1970, Africa Traditional Religion and Christianity, in A New Look at Christianity in Africa, Vol. II No.2.p16 Geneva: WSCF

23. Lincoln, Charles, Eric `,1974, Black Experience in Religion.
NY. Doubleday'

24. Mazrui, Ali Al' Amin ,1974; World Culture and the Black
Experience. Seattle: University of Washington Press.

25. Mbiti , John;,1969 African Religions and Philosophy.
Nairobi; Heinemann

26.National Geographic Society, Washington, D.C., Continental
Statistics

27. Ngugi Wa Thiongo, 1967,`Home Coming'
Nairobi; Heinemann

28. Ogot, Alan Bethwell and Rev. F.B. Welbourn 1966,A Place to Feel at Home' Nairobi:. Press

29.. Odinga, Oginga -1968; Not Yet Uhuru., An Autography Nairobi; Heinemann

30. .Ottenberg, Simon and Phoebe , 1960; Cultures and Societies of Africa NY: Random House

31.. Ploski, Harry ;, 1971,AfroUSA; A Reference work on the Black Experience ;Bellwether Publishing Co.'

32. Richardson, Harry V. , 1947; The Dark Glory. A Picture of the Church Among Negroes in the Rural South; NY: Friendship Press

33.. Ross, Emory and Myrta s, 1959,Africa Disturbed ..NY: Friendship Press

34.Sithole,Rev.Ndambaningi,1959,African Nationalism,

London; Oxford University Press

35. Slater, Mary,1968 The Caribbean Islands p.6-8, NY; Vikings Press.

36 Thomas, Tofori-Atta G.B. 1977- Liberation and Unity

Atlanta: Lantern Devotional   Booklet.

37.World Almanac.,2016; Information on Religious Affiliation.

.

ABOUT THE AUTHOR

The Revd. Prof. Dr. Nehemy Ndirangu Kihara was born in Nanyuki in Laikipia County of Kenya, East Africa.

He was educated at Timau in Meru County and Nairobi before graduating with a Licentiate of Theological Education from St. Paul's University (United Theological College), Limuru in Kiambu County.

He holds a Bachelor of Theology (B.Th.) in Biblical Literature and Geographic History from Christian International College.

He graduated with honors and attained a Master of Divinity (M.Div.) in Social Ethics, Psychology of Religion and Counseling, from the Interdenominational Theological Center at the Clark Atlanta University Complex.

He also attained a Doctor of Philosophy (Ph.D.) in Anthropology, Sociology of Religion and Political Science from Emory University.

As an Investigative Journalist and Radio Broadcaster this Independent Publisher hosted a weekend English and still hosts a weekly Swahili Community Show for Sagal Radio Services at WATB 1420 AM Station in Decatur, GA.

As an Interdisplinary Educator he taught Security Management and Police Studies for the Institute of Peace and Security Studies, (now known as the Department of Security and Correctional Science) of Kenyatta University in Nanyuki Campus, where he was the Coordinator of Humanities and Examinations Officer.

The Author also taught Introductory Psychology, Sociology, Criminal Procedure and Law of Evidence, Intelligence-Led Policing, Public Administration and General Management Principles among other units at the Nyeri and Embu Campuses.

He was an Adjunct Professor of Sociology/ Social Sciences at the Atlanta Campus of Saint Leo University, Tampa, Fl. Taught such courses as Anthropology, Sociology, and Criminal Justice units as Social Theory,

Drugs and Society, Marriage and Family, Research Methods, Human Behavior, among others He was an Adjunct Professor of Ethics at the Georgia Campus (Henry Medical Center) of the College of Health, University of St. Francis, Joliet, Ill.,

The Author was also the founding Moderating Bishop of the Ujamaa Nomadic Church -Without Borders, as a new church- mission initiative in US. He had also been an Urban Renewal/ Organizing Pastor of Beth Salem United Presbyterian Church, Columbus, Georgia. He served as an International Missionary in California, Iowa and New York, under the Mission to US program of the Presbyterian Church, USA.

As a Senior Lecturer at Kenyatta University, the Author taught African Culture, Belief Systems, Social Theory and Research Methods units in the Department of Philosophy and Religious Studies and also in the Department of Sociology. He was also an Activist Educator, who fought for academic freedom and excellence, which led to his unfair dismissal by the government which controlled the public universities and educational institutions.

Reverend Professor Ndirangu Kihara started his career a high school teacher and principal at Muthithi Secondary School, and then an ordained Church Minister of Muthithi Parish and the Stated Clerk of the wider Murang'a Presbytery of the Presbyterian Church of East Africa.

BLUERGREEN PUBLISHING

www.ingramcontent.com/pod-product-compliance
Lightning Source LLC
Chambersburg PA
CBHW060155290526
45789CB00003B/1046